The Ultimate Guide to Manifestation

9 Magical Ways to Manifest
Your Heart's Desires

Suresh Harvu

Copyright © 2016 by Suresh Harvu
www.ultimateguidetomanifestation.com
www.manifestingchambers.com

All rights reserved. No part of this publication may be reproduced, distributed, or transmitted in any form or by any means, including photocopying, recording, or other electronic or mechanical methods, without the prior written permission of the publisher except for the use of brief quotations in a book review.

The information provided in this book is not intended to be a treatment or a prescription for any bodily issues. It is intended to be used at the sole discretion of the reader.

Printed in Canada
First Printing, 2016
ISBN: 978-1-77277-016-2

10-10-10 Publishing
Markham, Ontario
CANADA

Contents

Foreword	v
Acknowledgements	vii
The Foundation	1
Chapter 1: How Does Manifestation Really Work?	7
Chapter 2: Philosophy Behind 9 Chambers and Your Preparedness to See Miracles	15
Chapter 3: The First Chamber - The Magic of Believing and Intention	23
Chapter 4: The Second Chamber - The Magic of Visualization and Feeling	33
Chapter 5: The Third Chamber - The Magic of The Power of Silence	43
Chapter 6: The Fourth Chamber - The Magic of Vibrations	51
Chapter 7: The Fifth Chamber - The Magic of Universal Quantum Influence	59
Chapter 8: The Sixth Chamber - The Magic of The Power of I Am That I Am	69

Chapter 9: The Seventh Chamber - The Magic of Positive Action   75

Chapter 10: The Eighth Chamber - The Magic of 40 Day Chunking   83

Chapter 11: The Ninth Chamber - The Magic of Celebration and Sharing   89

Q&A   93

Appendix   97

About the Author   100

Foreword

Do you sometimes feel discouraged or frustrated about not having achieved anything significant in your life? Is there a sense of hopelessness and leaving your future at the mercy of fate?

Understanding manifestation will always be a challenge for you, if you have not been exposed to a systematic plan. Without a clear direction, you will be running in circles. To be truly happy, you must be in a position to use your unique talents and natural gifts to add value to your own life and to the lives of others.

Clarity leads to power, and eventually to success. You need to understand the basics of how things show up in your life and why. Suresh Harvu has done a wonderful job in his book, The Ultimate Guide to Manifestation. He distills the whole manifestation process into 9 direct, practical steps that you should follow if you aspire to achieve something significant in your life. He has a knack of making a complex topic look achievable within a very short span of time, and he is passionate about teaching the various methods. You now have a choice to set your goals high and get down to the basics of manifesting, as prescribed in this book.

To your achievements,

Raymond Aaron
NY Times Bestselling Author

Acknowledgements

I would like to offer gratitude and hymns from my heart to my eternal Guru Paramahansa Yogananda (www.yogananda-srf.org) who has instilled in me the meaning and understanding of this game called Life. All inspiration to anything in this Life has come from Him. His book *The Autobiography of a Yogi* is a boon to mankind.

My sincere thanks and gratitude to Dr. Anil Nanduri (www.drnanduri.com) who has shown me what passion is all about in helping people. I know for sure that Dr Anil has a healing touch that comes straight from his intention to help people out of their sufferings. My meeting with him for the first time in New Jersey 14 years ago was one of the Universal winks that I explain in this book.

I would like to thank Balram Chinta, Sr Technical Architect at AT&T for his high motivation and selfless attitude of serving others in the community. He has been an inspiration for me to do the best in any endeavor that I undertake.

I would like to thank Dr. Robert Field (http://www.resonanceschoolofhomeopathy.com/) for his outstanding interpretations of Spiritual Homeopathy provided through his practical cases offered in his school. Being a student of Dr. Robert for the last 5 years has helped me immensely in understanding and implementing the concept of an ***"unprejudiced observer"*** in my daily life of dealing with individuals from various backgrounds.

The Foundation

You have listened to a small inner voice that makes you believe that this book might make a difference in your life. I do not know your inner strengths or your level (aka Vibrational Quotient that you will learn in this book) of understanding of why things do happen the way they happen. I would be doing a disservice if I take you through this book without providing you a foundation on which the whole book is built. Through my interaction with people from various backgrounds and in the process of me guiding individuals for the last 15 years, I have found that each person's needs are different, their priorities in life change multiple times and most of them come with a preconceived mindset about anything they encounter. I do not assume anything. You might have never come across a book like this before or it is possible you might have heard but you were not drawn towards the principles. Or you might be the one who is well aware of your circumstances and why they are so and you would like to bring about a huge change and are ready to acquire the knowledge, the tools and a plan to make it happen.

This chapter will provide you with a very broad foundation that I would encourage you to study and let it soak into your inner space. I have been a student for the last 25 years, always eager to know the intricacies of the working of the Universe and have accumulated lot of notable successes in the areas close to my heart. You can read and listen to me on my site www.ultimateguidetomanifestation.com.

You could use this chapter as a "Life 101" that would make you ready for the nuts and bolts throughout this book. I believe that this chapter by itself can give you a major shift in paradigm to look at things a bit differently than you are probably used to. Jim Rohn once said - "You have only one life to live in this lifetime. Do something and keep exploring. You might come to know your purpose here."

I present here below some of the most important takeaways that will give you a framework within which you start your exploration and expand your horizons to become a true and gifted manifestor.

7 Major Universal Principles

1. The Universe and the entire cosmos runs on the energy of **LOVE**. Love is the binding agent between couples, families, cultures, nations and the myriads of Universes physically floating in the depths of tranquility.

2. The Universe is a very patient and forgiving teacher. With the human kind having the exclusive power of choice, no one can make you do anything that you do not choose. Every moment of your life is a choice from the infinity of choices you are offered. You feel like some choices are not what you intended but that is the fallacy of the ego mind that keeps working trying to justify every single choice or decision. You can always start afresh, draw a line and change.

3. Everything in the Universe moves, vibrates and travels in circular patterns, the same principles of vibration in the physical world apply to our thoughts, feelings, desires and wills in the Etheric world. Each sound, thing, and even thought has its own vibrational frequency, unique unto itself.

4. The Universe is continually growing with unlimited resources with effortless ease. Creation is constant and predictable based on the energy of the seed planted, the thoughts, words and the vibrations.

5. Everything we see and experience in the external world has its origin in the invisible, mental realm. So it means that every cause has an effect and every effect has a cause.

6. Everything is dual and has poles. Everything has its pair of opposites; opposites are identical in nature, but different in degree. It means that there are two sides to everything. Things that appear as opposites are in fact only two extremes of the same thing. For instance, heat and cold may appear to be opposites at first glance, but in truth they are simply varying degrees of the same thing called temperature. The same applies to love and hate, peace and war, positive and negative, good and evil, yes and no, light and darkness, energy and matter. You can transform your thoughts from hate to love, from fear to courage by consciously raising your vibrations. This is what is called the Art of Polarization.

7. Desire, belief and expectations have a tendency to become a self-fulfilling prophecy. When one expects with confidence that good things will happen, they usually will and this holds true the other way around.

9 Major Life Matters

1. Life is always a **fair** game. The earlier one understands, the better the fairness shows up in one's life.

2. There are no accidents in life. Nothing happens by chance or outside the Universal Laws. When you become the observer of the unfolding moments in your life, it would not be a mystery to **connect the dots** that lead you from one event to another, from one circumstance to another. This book shows you how to choose those moments from the limitless possibilities.

3. It takes a minute to change your life. It is that moment when you declare to your inner self and the Universe that you are now in

charge of your life and would do whatever it takes to jump - a quantum jump upward and forward in the pursuit of your life journey.

4. Life of gratitude makes the Universe bend to manage your successes. This is one indicator that can mark your life as special and worth living to enjoy the journey. It is not giving thanks for all the pleasant experiences you go through, but it is a gratitude for your life itself and that includes your environment, circumstances, family, the ups and downs and all that makes this game called life.

5. Each person receives a series of situations or lessons for the purpose of strengthening the light within. Each of these situations is a challenge to remain connected to our hearts when proceeding to solve the problems.

6. Success manifests overnight but the preparation always is structured and precedes it.

7. Nothing in this life lasts forever except the Love you have generated and shared and the path that you engraved by being in resonance to Universal principles.

8. The attitude towards life determines life's attitude towards you. The game of life has a very unique way of providing you what you put out to the Universe.

9. You are born as a spiritual being having a human existence and not the other way round. This is why you are challenged to recreate yourself in the highest vision you had about yourself.

Physical Universe vs Spiritual Universe

1. It takes an EFFORT to produce physical realities by your labor in the physical world while everything FLOWS effortlessly in the spiritual world.

2. There are two ways to make something happen. One is by struggle in the physical world and the other is by postulating in the spiritual world. This book will help you postulate more consistently by high energy, word choice, knowing that you can get things effortlessly and by your own inner transformation.

3. There is always a concept of time, energy and space involved for any physical act while it is totally absent in the spiritual universe. We live in a world that is consciously and unconsciously enslaved by the illusionary mental paradigm we call "time". Not understanding this truth is the reason why someone has difficulty in understanding the so called accidents in life. Understanding and coming to a point of knowing will bring in the explanation of all the Universal winks (the word accidents now gets replaced by the more powerful word "synchronicity") that take place in your life.

I would strongly encourage you to become an inquisitive traveler in your journey. There must be an all-pervading intelligence that is the backbone of all creation. But with this *difference* - that man is an active part of this Universal Mind. He partakes of its creative wisdom and power and that by working in harmony with this Universal Mind, he can create anything, have anything, be anything that his heart secretly desires.

When the student is ready, the teacher appears--A Buddhist proverb

Chapter 1

HOW DOES MANIFESTATION REALLY WORK?

WHAT IS MANIFESTATION?

Is it not strange to even think about the word manifest? Why should anyone even entertain this idea that there is something mysterious behind this word? What do you think? Are you one of those who shrug it off as a concept or are you saying to yourself "these things do not work", or how about "people make a fool of others with this law of attraction craze", or "maybe it is true but I just cannot do all these as I have other important things to do"? Or are you willing to question yourself like; " I know this will work but how do I really go about", or "There are so many people talking, writing and babbling about this, I am not sure which one to follow", or "I do see and hold in my hands a step by step approach, I think I can do it and let me give my 110%. What do I lose or better what do I actually gain"?

So let's get to the question that is being asked here. What is manifestation all about and where do I go from here?

The simplest definition of this word I find in the Merriam-Webster is:
- sign that shows something clearly
- one of the forms that something has when it appears or occurs

Yes, it is a sign one receives that something is appearing in their sphere of influence within their own environment. It could be as tangible as a car, a house, a vacation, a job, a spouse, an ulcer in the stomach or even a business card that someone exchanged. Or it could be as intangible as a feeling within oneself of well-being or otherwise, a deep love building up for a person or community. So, if you have been part of this experience anytime in the recent past or anytime in your life, then the question that is really called for is: Did I manifest all these things or was it a random roll of dice in the game of life that brought forth these objects?

Before you proceed to read further, just close your eyes for a few minutes (don't get surprised if you get pulled into a vicious circle of thoughts... we will get that taken care soon. I promise you!) and try to answer yourself in as much detail as possible ,the following questions. Do not judge anyone or anything. Just let your thoughts and memory unwind a few things that have already taken place in your space.

What is it that I have acquired recently that is tangible? You might have paid for it or someone might have gifted it to you or you might have just found it. How did it come to me and what is the chain of events that took place for me to acquire this thing? Go back as much as you can to get the whole chain of events.

What is an unpleasant experience or object that you experienced or acquired recently like a job that you hate, or a boss that you don't like working with, or a health issue that looks like it is cropping up almost overnight, or an accident you were involved with, or an argument that you had with your spouse or a parent or a child? Go back as much as you can to get to the chain of events that took place leading to this experience.

Make sure you get your mind working on the above before proceeding further. If you need time, place a book mark here on this page and come back. My goal for this book is to help you achieve your heart's desires. So please bear with me if I ask you to do some action steps.
If nothing came up so far, great...let's continue. If you took the action step and did go back down memory lanes, you did come up with something. Keep that in your current space for now.

Let me share one such experience that my mind took me on. It happened not long ago..In fact it was just yesterday the 1st of January 2016 when I encountered a gas leak in our cooking range after pulling it out for a good new year cleaning to remove all the small things that have fallen behind the gas range. As anyone who knows about gas, it is always a scary thing to even think about it as faulty. Had I not pulled it, may be nothing would have happened. There is no end to these "Had I .." or " I should not have.." .. Right? Was there a panic attack or did I take suitable immediate action or did I cut my new year mood off by saying "Is this the way my new year began...what is in store all year long?" I could justify each one of my responses and I would have all the "OMG.." " it is terrible..." from all near and dear.. Right? You still with me? Of course I called the emergency gas leak (it is good to keep the number handy), got them to confirm the leak, tried fixing the issue myself with the help of my dear friend, got it tested again to have found another leak , got a licensed gas fitter now to work on it, paying a nice, unexpected amount of money and finally after a 24 hour mini drama, the cooking was back with full vigor and taste.

Did I call for all this so called trouble and how in the world I could manifest or bring forth this event? I will come back to this later in the book when I arm you with the right armor. Ask the same question to the happenings at your end and see if you could answer. If you are one of those studious readers, go write down the answer you think it is.

The question again for a recap is: Did you call for or manifest the experiences or things be it a pleasant one or an unpleasant one? There is no wrong or right answer to start with but by the end of this book, I hope you will be able to sit back and answer the question slightly differently that would make perfect sense to you.

So let's make a point here and a premise before we dig into the how to and the mechanics of manifestation:

Everything going on in your life is a manifestation process culminating into something tangible or intangible.

My goal for you is to direct this process in such a way that the end result is something that you have truly set your heart to. This is a very ambitious statement to make, but for now I would urge you to trust the process in order for you to continue from here while letting the message sink in without any intentional blocking.

WHY IS IT THEN SO DIFFICULT TO FULFILL OUR HEART's DESIRES IF WE ARE THE ONES TO MANIFEST?

Good question to ask right? You can nod your head. That would actually help you in the process.

Is it just that the Law of Attraction (if you have been lucky to hear about this term) works for some and not for the other unlucky ones? Or did someone ask you to watch the movie "The Secret" multiple times so that you start attracting what you truly desire? While the Law of Attraction and the Secret are truly phenomenal, it would be unwise to hold the view that they work only for some or it is just a fluke that someone meets his desires head on and you are still sitting on the fence watching the birds snatch away your desires and fly away. In fact if you have not watched the movie "The Secret," it would be a good time alongside this book to watch. May be that could become the triggering point in your quest for manifestation.

The reason the law of attraction does not work for the majority of people who attempt is because they don't understand the difference between having a heartfelt desire and achieving it which is mostly a habitual and emotional process. It is all about how you train both parts of the brain; the logical and the creative parts to be in coherence to form a matrix that leads to the fulfillment of desires. If this reasoning jumps over your head, take heart. You are not alone and in the pages ahead the whole process would bring clarity.

WHY DO WE NEED A STEP BY STEP PLAN TO MANIFEST OUR HEART'S DESIRES?

With the brief introduction above, I think it is time to get to a more practical understanding of the term manifestation. If you do not get a good grasp of this term, the steps and the process itself might start looking vague. After all you do not want this to become a concept but to be a real practical approach to manifest your heart's desires.

Here is my definition of manifestation based on years of refining the process that I am offering in this book.

It is; "A systematic approach using Universal Laws for a realistic attainment of a desire that is truly empowering for the betterment of oneself and/or others."

While I lay out the whole process in front of the reader in the pages ahead, let us be clear as to what the "realistic attainment of a desire" really entails.

Let's say you desire ("want" is a word you should do your best to be away from !!!) to make an extra $50,000.00, $100,000.00, or even $1 million dollars. Or let's say that you desire to shed the extra 40 pounds weight around your favorite area in your body. Or let's say that you desire to find a soul mate (assuming you are not with one now!!!) . Do you really, really, really desire these things or is it a good wish to have and write it down in your favorite goal book? If you are earning say $20,000 now, does your mind and heart truly believe you can get to the magic figure of a million? If so, you are awesome!! We will get to it sooner than you think with the process that you will embark upon. If not, let's do a bit of re-thinking in the desire list. How about shedding an extra 5 pounds out of the 40 pounds you initially desired? Are you ready to put the process to a test? If so, welcome to the land of magical ways to manifest your heart's desires. Get that 5 pounds off or get that extra $10000 and then set yourself up to a higher desire and you in your heart and mind would truly understand the tested process that you could take it to any levels you NOW truly desire. I would encourage my readers to test out the waters (the process here) with an open heart (please do not go to your doctor now for an open heart!!!).

People see the future as an uncertainty waiting hopefully that it will bring to them what they wish for. But the current moment was the future of our past and the future will be the result of our present. Every moment in our life, we are weaving the threads that will make the cloth of our future. So it stands to reason to hold on to the present and drive the moments going forward for fulfillment, for success, for that deep rooted accomplishments.

Yes, you can do it. There is no price to be paid for believing in yourself and letting you submerge into the magical chambers gifted in this book. In the same vein, there could be a big price to be paid for not believing in yourself. That price could take various forms like despair, hopelessness, anxiety, stress, ill-health, mediocrity or it could be that sentence that you would not really speak on your last bed: "I wish I had done something better. I wish I had lived my life fully for myself and my loved ones". Allow me to take you on this magical journey. Stick to this plan like crazy glue, and you will see that the Universe sticks to you bringing forth all the goodness you are worthy of.

"Clarity is Power", says Anthony Robbins. And when you have a proven, systematized step by step approach to magically manifest your heart's desires, you get total clarity in what needs to be done. Your desires can be manifested. As you turn the pages with hope in your heart and the confidence in the process, keep in mind that the desires you have are YOURS. Let that not get diluted. If you are not sure what your desires should be, allow me to guide you through the whole journey. I promise the journey will be worth traveling and will be worth your time and effort. At the end of this journey, you would look back and say:

"Wow... this book was something that I manifested and it turned out into a gold mine of personal fulfillment."

Suresh Harvu

MY EXPERIENCES SO FAR

Chapter 2

PHILOSOPHY BEHIND 9 CHAMBERS AND YOUR PREPAREDNESS TO SEE MIRACLES

There is one important step we need to take before proceeding through the 9 magical chambers. I can understand that you are too eager to rush through them as you want to see what is at the end of the journey. We all are guilty of wanting, but are not even sure what are we looking for. What we are trying to accomplish here is not just a fancy wish but a desire fulfilled that would become a triggering point for astounding success in all fields. As you complete this important step, you would be ready to go through the 9 chambers one at a time. I have promised myself to remind the reader that what he or she holds is a book that is meant to transform the lives of generations to come.

You will come back time and again each time with a different latent desire to be fulfilled, by going through the pages laid out in this book. You will also see the number 9 appearing in many of the action steps. There seems to be something astonishing about this number (may be 10 looks too big for some; the reason why the prices in the stores or gas stations end with .99 cents). It could be accomplishing something in 9-minute bursts or 9-minute milestones or 9-minute cardio workout per weekday adding up to roughly one full work week per year to focus on your goals and dreams. So let's stick to this 9 magical number to progress from here.

So let's begin:

Do you have a desire or a goal or a dream that you would like to see fulfilled? Do you believe in having one?

Let me ask you a question. Have you ever bought a house to own or to rent? If so, you must have first thought of buying or renting and then visiting the housing market and bought or rented it outright and started living there happily ever after.

If that sounds absurd, then most likely you must have:

Thought of buying or renting a house, scanned through housing sites or found a realtor and gave the requirements and the budget, visited and inspected the house in the neighborhood you preferred, had a time frame before which you bought or rented and finally decided on a particular property.

There could have been many more factors in between that you must have thought of before going through the process. Now, just imagine if buying a property or a house had to go through so much planning and effort, don't you think building a life would need some sort of planning and preparedness?

The trouble with not having a goal is that you can spend your life running up and down the field and never score. There are two primary choices in life: to accept conditions as they exist, or accept the responsibility for changing them.

Hopefully, you are somewhat convinced about a need to build up a desire in your heart and not let your life run on autopilot and at the end of the day make statements like; "The economy is terrible..." or "I got so unlucky." or " I have been brought up by my family who did not provide anything to me." or "The rich gets richer anyway through unfair means." or any of those excuses that you could justify. By the very fact that you are holding this book and reading these words, I truly believe you are not one of them.

The Ultimate Guide to Manifestation

Welcome to the land of visions, dreams, goals and desires. And let us go head on to be prepared to receive. Here is a very small exercise that I would like you to do before going through the chambers to activate your desires. Without this exercise (I promise you it might take as little as 2 minutes or it might take a whole weekend….we will see!!) it is going to be of little use attempting to understand and master the how to's in the coming chapters.

I am very serious about you achieving your heartfelt desires. Are you having the same commitment to achieve your goals in a systematic way that the world will term it as "magical?" It is almost like going to the train ticket booth and asking for a train route without mentioning the destination. So I urge, request, beg and maybe demand your participation in the exercise NOW!! Treat yourself as the captain of your Life ship. Demand of yourself the very best and boldly demand of Life ship to accept your commands. The method of demanding though is a bit different here that you are about to embark upon. So let's get to the bottom line.

a. Use the table provided below for this exercise.

b. Take a good sharp pencil and an eraser along with it. You might need to use them more than once. Go get one before going to the next step.

c. Close your eyes for just 60 seconds and take a deep inhalation from your nose to let your stomach push outwards and while exhaling, relax your body from the head to the toe. Do this 2 or 3 times.. We will go over this in detail in an upcoming chamber.

d. Write down under each of the category mentioned in the space provided, just ONE heartfelt desire (that you have not yet achieved but are yearning for it) that you are accomplishing (Remember… no wanting to achieve…you are! And please don't put a thought on how you are going to achieve.). If you have trouble writing, close your eyes again for 30 seconds, breathe in and relax, open your eyes and start writing.

SPIRITUALITY	FAMILY	HEALTH	FINANCE	CAREER/PERSONAL

Here are some pointers just to let your creative juices start flowing.

SPIRITUALITY :

One can be highly spiritual and not religious. So open your mind and let it act like a parachute that works only when it is open. Some desires could be :

- giving charity of $1000 this year to help needy people
- Waking up in the morning at 5 am and doing 30 minutes of meditation
- helping 5 economically deprived kids with their education

FAMILY :

This includes relationship with spouse, kids, parents etc. Some desires could be:

- Spend 15 minutes each day with your kids playing with them.
- Planning a vacation to Greece with the family and making it fun
- Learn piano or guitar along with your spouse or kids

HEALTH :

This includes maintaining good health and/or getting rid of chronic health issues. Some desires could be:

- Be physically and energetically fit by maintaining an optimal weight of 150 pounds
- Drink wheat grass juice every day for good nutrition
- Run a minimum of 10 miles a week to keep the heart in perfect condition
- Totally adapting to the seasonal changes while maintaining perfect immune system
- Totally get rid of the chronic knee pain or any other troublesome issue in the body

FINANCES :

The goal would normally be to increase current earning capacity and/or find new sources of income generation. Some desires could be:

- Increase income by 25% over last year in order to fulfill your desire to help your family and the needy
- Start a part time business to augment income that would add an extra $5000 every month
- Have at least 3 sources of income
- Maintain a cash flow record of all expenditures to plug those that are not needed

PERSONAL:

Some desires could be:

- Keep at least 3 sets of good clothes that improve your self esteem and attitude

- Start writing a journal once a week
- Always have a high energy outlook with positive affirmations
- Surprise spouse or kids at irregular intervals to make life more fun to live and enjoy

CAREER :

Some desires could be:

- Learn one extra skill that would help in the job market
- Become a mentor to someone at work in the area of expertise
- Get promotion at work by giving value to the team and to the company
- Get out of the mechanical job life and replace income by doing what is passionate

The heartfelt desires you are going to write are not Ego based but Soul based. What this really means is that the purpose of the desires is to give you fulfillment and an opportunity to serve others. Soul based desires are the ones that tap into the magical zone while ego based desires tap into fear and uncertainty .If you have completed writing in the box, go through each of them very slowly and let the desire sink in now. If you feel in your heart that there is another burning desire than the one you wrote, go ahead and erase it and write the new one. At the end of this exercise, you SHOULD be able to clearly tell what your heartfelt desires are that you are achieving in a very short period of 12 to 24 months.

Good Job so far! This start is really half the job. Your mind and your heart have underlined the most important desires and you have in fact started the churning process in the ether. You are already in the top 8% of the population who actually know what they intently desire and not just a wavering want or wish. Believe that you have put yourself way ahead of the game right in this chapter. So here is a sentence I would like you to think while reading, and if possible, write it down in your journal.

Nine magical chambers there are that I know. By divine grace I will pass through each and let the magic flow. My heartfelt desires are so pure in my heart...I am letting the nine chambers work its magic and set me apart.

Suresh Harvu

MY EXPERIENCES SO FAR

Chapter 3

THE FIRST CHAMBER - THE MAGIC OF BELIEVING AND INTENTION

MAGIC OF BELIEVING

Finally, we are here after your first attempt at listing out clearly what you intend to achieve in the next 1, 2 or 5 years from now. Welcome to the very first chamber in the process of manifesting your heart's desires. I hope by this time you have clearly laid out what you are expecting to achieve in a reasonably short span of time.

Have you ever heard or read about how a coach takes an inferior football or baseball team and infuse them with something that causes them to go out and win game after game. In the same vein, you must have read about how Warren Buffet and other investors smile at the market meltdown and come out richer than before while others lose their investments complaining about the same. Such stories are inspirational due to the fact these people have come out from nowhere with hardly anything to boast of, and are now in the limelight sharing and encouraging the masses. It all comes down to a single thread that can be termed as **BELIEF**.

Belief is that single word and power, that causes people to be cured through mental healing, lets others climb the ladder of success in whatever field they choose, and for others, gets phenomenal results. There is something magical about believing, though it cannot be satisfactorily explained to the mind that questions it in the first place and is not ready for possibility thinking. The world around us is a mirror to the beliefs we harbor within ourselves.

No mind ever receives the truth until it is prepared to receive it.

The book you are holding now is the outcome of belief in the first place followed by a series of steps that you will uncover in the chapters ahead. Pattern of life is altered to the person who begins with a belief in the first place that he or she can accomplish the desires listed out from the heart.

The core belief is what propels you to achieve your goals. When you achieve them, it could be termed as a coincidence by the so called experts on everything. It could be people very close to you, but you and you alone would be the one smiling from within, knowing what it has taken to achieve them. As you go through this powerful belief session and follow through the steps laid out, you would be tempted to let others know. I would encourage you to keep that attitude of sharing, but at the same time be conscious about to whom you are addressing. It all starts with an open mind.

This subject of belief can become a book by itself, and I would like to address here the belief that it takes for you to take the next step.

It is all about saying: "That could be done" instead of "Not sure that could be done". It is the power of suggestion, be it autosuggestion (the one you own to yourself) or heterosuggestion (the one coming to you from outside of yourself) that starts the magic of believing in you causing the subconscious to begin creating the magical creative work. This is where the power of affirmations and incantations come into play. It is the time taken from the point of non belief to the point where the belief becomes a deep conviction when things begin to happen.

To succeed on any scale, we have to dismiss the false beliefs (or non belief) of the past. There is a need to believe that we can control to a very large extent whatever happens in our life and that we can make a difference in our world. It is like a thermostat that regulates just what we accomplish in life. You will be astonished as to the way you walk, talk, discuss and act by changing your belief thermostat and set it to a higher level while the subconscious keeps up with the level you set. The subconscious picks up on your beliefs like a magnet, and so you have every reason to fill your mind with positive beliefs about being able to achieve your goal. Your subconscious is always creating your life based on your beliefs.

As you would explore ahead, everything in this world has an energy vibration attached to it. You would direct your energy vibration upward to be climbing steadily, as you move from the position you are in now to the position you desire to be in a few months and years from now. Disbelief is negative power. When the mind disbelieves or doubts, the mind attracts 'reasons' to support the disbelief.

What you believe in your heart is what you attract

Action steps:
Go back to the desires you listed out in the previous chapter and read them out loud to yourself. Remember, you are in this by yourself to start with. At the expense of redundancy, let me again gently remind you why you are here. It is your desires that you would like to materialize. It is the magic you are creating in your life. You are doing whatever it takes for a very short period to see for yourself achieving your heartfelt desires. The world will watch your caravan takeoff.

The "how to do it" ALWAYS comes to the person who BELIEVES "HE CAN DO IT."

I hope you are still in this game and that you are going to cross the finish line.

Here are 4 action steps you can take right now to increase your belief vibration.

Make sure you have five to ten minutes of pure undivided attention each and every day to follow these steps.

1. Close your eyes and place your awareness on the center of your forehead. Just think success, whatever that means to you at this point. As softly and slowly as you can, repeat 9 times silently in your mind - *"I BELIEVE I am a success. I BELIEVE I am succeeding. I BELIEVE in my capacity to achieve."* When the small ugly inner voice raises its head and tries to negate your power of belief, just say; "Thank you for sharing" and continue with the exercise.

2. For each of the desires you have listed, make an affirmation about achieving it. For instance, if your desire was to make an extra $20000 dollars this year, mentally affirm: *"I am making $20000 over and above what I am making now. I know and I believe that this is happening. Opportunities are knocking on my door as I speak."* Try not to shortcut this approach. Do this for each of the desires. Your goal is to get this in your head within a week without the need to refer to your list.

3. Imagine that it is six months or a year from now and you have manifested everything you had desired. Try to picture it. The dream job you desired, the million dollar idea you got and acted upon, the pregnancy you had wished for a long time, the morning jog you always desired is now second nature to you. It sounds too good to believe. Right? You better start believing NOW.

4. Now let go of the thoughts you just created, affirmed and imagined. Trust that you have already set the process in motion.

MAGIC OF INTENTON

Everything that is created in the universe is here already. We are not really creators as much as we are co-creators or re-combiners of everything. It is the intention behind our thoughts that traps the required energies into manifesting the objects we desire.

Change the way you look at things and the things you look at will change. Intention is all about allowing things to happen. It cannot be forced or demanded. It is the starting point in the attraction process.

While belief is a knowing that you are capable of achieving, intention is the creative power you employ to bring the desire to fruition, whether for money, relationships, spirituality or love. Most of us would have had a firsthand experience with this power. You might have been thinking about buying a Land Rover and researching all about this car. When you go to the dealer to get some quotes and lo and behold, you would find Land Rovers on the road at very frequent intervals. It was always there, but your intention, your creative force brought that object in front of you. It is not a chance or a coincidence that some might be tempted to think that way. It is literally co-creating the circumstances that you intend to attract. When you set an intention and then act on it to demonstrate your commitment, amazing things occur.

This little known magic of intention has been instrumental in my life in so many ways. It has helped me in my energy healing work with amazing results.

Here is an example of a few of the hundreds of text message I receive. A client of mine went through an energy healing session for her severe backache. She had called me with agonizing pain in her back unable to move . I put myself into a meditative state, put my intention to the Universe that the energy that I am passing is landing at the right place (she was 8000 miles away) and that she is healed. I also thanked in advance to the Universe, the field of infinite possibilities, for the healing done.

She writes: "The healing has worked very well. I never had this experience before. I drank lots of water with intentions and it has been just pure magic all the while. I was able to walk for 1.5 hours absolutely without my back pain. This is truly awesome."

A few more messages from others that will drive home the point of the magic of **intention**:

"I am doing **intentions** the way you asked me to do. Today the swelling in my leg and pain has reduced by almost 50 percent. Thank you so much."

"I taught my mom the water **intention** you taught me for her sleepless nights since long. She slept very well last night after such a long time. It is all magic happening everywhere. Thanks a zillion."

"The **intentions** are working for my husband. Thank you the awesome session we had."

"My dad never believed in meditation. But since I am doing the **intentions** every day, he has started doing it for the first time in his life."

Action steps:

"Our intention creates our reality." ~Wayne Dyer

Here are 4 action steps to tap into this magic of intention. By this time, I hope you are a bit more familiar with the list you created earlier. It is a good idea to go back and read them once aloud. You are being trained and led into the chambers one step at a time.

a. Create an intention statement for each of the items in your list and write them down on two index cards. Keep one at all times with you wherever you go, and the other keep it in a drawer near your bed side. Here are a few examples that you could build your intention list upon:

- **I intend to** generate an extra $50000 this year by pursuing my passion.
- **I intend to** completely get rid of my knee pain and be able to run a mile each day.
- **I intend to** create a massive passive income of at least $10000 per month from 3 sources, that would help me and my family for generations to come to live an abundant life.
- **I intend to** create a beautiful relationship with my spouse that would set an example for my kids on what true love is.

b. One of the most effective tools to release this power is through silence. Close your eyes gently and put your awareness on the center of your forehead. Just watch your breath going in and coming out. Relax and repeat this step a couple of times.

c. For each item in your list, say the intention silently, slowly and gently within, and then mentally release the intention and desire. Just stop thinking about it. Releasing the intention out will merge it with infinite possibilities to attract the right resources.

d. During your waking state, your inner voice might raise its ugly head to deter you from moving forward with the steps outlined. It could be that other people's doubts might try to creep into your inner mind. Remember, you and your inner self knows better. Move forward by just acknowledging those distractions with a silent "Thank you for sharing."

Let the intention work its magic on you. Do not force or question or attach yourself to a specific event or result. Just keep the intention intact by practicing the steps daily. Opportunities and circumstances will start flowing towards you.

Keep a note of how you felt while exercising the magic of belief and intention.

> ***When you set an intention and you commit,***
> ***the whole universe conspires.***

The Ultimate Guide to Manifestation

MY EXPERIENCES SO FAR

Chapter 4

THE SECOND CHAMBER - THE MAGIC OF VISUALIZATION AND FEELING

WHY VISUALIZATON AND FEELING ARE POWERFUL

You are now ready to take another major step towards your desires. This chamber of Visualization and Feeling is likely the most important and potent chamber designed to create the necessary blueprint for the limitless possibilities for the design and manifestation of your heart's desires. We live in an ocean of vibrating energy that is always responding to how and what we think. Each moment in our life is an expression of a vibrant force known as thoughts. Our thoughts have the power to let the grand quantum Universe design our lives with clarity and purpose.

You could use this process of visualization and feelings as a very potent tool in your journey. When you have this bucket list of things to be achieved, and you have set your belief thermostat at a reasonably high level of expectancy, and you have now combined that with a purposeful intention that has become a force in itself, you are ready to embark upon a journey that can take your intentions and make it into your inner reality. We easily forget that we are the controllers of our reality – and that "our reality" is not made up of outside influences, but it actually consists of our thoughts, beliefs and mindset.

What you believe with positive intent , see and feel about, you bring about.

It is all an inner game. Visualization is the ability to see things in the inner mind's eye much before they become an outside reality. The more you accept, trust and practice this process, the more you master the inner game. When you can produce realities in your inner mind, the manifestation process of harnessing the powers of the Universe kicks in to bring those inner images to your physical world. If you could burn into your memory and your daily life the statement below, you would be doing a great service to your future:

Your brain cannot differentiate between real action and mental action.

There has been so much research to prove this statement that there are volumes of evidence if one is keen to study them all. Instead, let us accept it with all the belief in our heart and do what is needed to go through this chamber of visualization and feeling and come out of it pleasantly surprised as to what it brings about. Yes, visualization is an art and can be perfected by practice. No one can honestly tell that they are not a visual person or they cannot visualize. It is a matter of putting oneself in the proper frame of mind before beginning to start this process. It is not a random fancy thing to do, that most of us tend to think of visualization to be . It is to be used as a tool and they do come with rules.

Here are a few requirements before you begin a Visualization exercise.

- Allocate a minimum of 5 minutes each and every day in a place where you are not disturbed.

- Complete a 2 minute relaxation process to place your body and mind in a position of receptivity. This is achieved by going into the Alpha state (as explained in the UGM Appendix A) wherein you are an active participant and become a co-creator in the manifestation process.

- Repeat the desire list silently and slowly in your mind and put your intention out. Use your index card until you have mastered them.

- Always end the session by bringing yourself back to the Beta state (refer UGM Appendix A)). This is a very important step, as one would love to drift off in the other state due to sheer joy and peace. In fact you are in touch with bliss as you move forward.

How does Feeling merge into this mix?

Before we create a step by step plan for visualization, let's look at how Feeling and Visualization are inter-related. Why are they both being addressed here in the same chamber? This is where people are stumped. I have heard stories about people following the Law of Attraction, and at the end they have only one thing to say ; "It does not work for me though I tried." In reality, it does work, provided you understand that behind all these visualizations, the Universe is looking for that Feeling of yours that goes along with achieving them. It is so similar to a combination lock wherein each number in the combination is important and has to correlate with the other.

We are conditioned in our world to have our feelings in response to something else that happens to us in our world. That feeling is a doorway to a power that lives within each of us. We have an inner technology and a power that we can remember and we can bring it to the forefront that would not only help us manifest all our heart's desires, but be a boon to this world full of chaos, suffering and uncertainty.

> *"Time does not flow just in one direction. The future exists simultaneously with the past." …..Einstein*

Let us take a few examples and I urge you to work with me full throttle. Read them one at a time and then close your eyes to demonstrate to yourself the power of feelings.

a. *Imagine you holding a nice juicy lemon in your hand. It is just ripe to be squeezed into juice. Imagine smelling it close to your nose and squeeze a bit. Feel the nice little puff of the juice touching your nose and some going into your mouth. Now slowly cut the lemon into two halves and take one half and now have the ultimate thrill of squeezing it into your mouth. Squeeze it till the last drop. Open your eyes.* Take a moment or two and go to the next example.

b. *Imagine yourself to be driving a car of your choice. You are in a mood to put this beast into action. You drive 100 miles per hour on a 50 mile limit zone. You are enjoying the speed, the drive and the acceleration. Keep driving for a minute. All of a sudden you see a cop's car right behind you with the red light swirling around. Open your eyes.* Take a moment or two and go to the next example.

c. *Imagine yourself sitting in the hot afternoon sun with a sun magnifier glass. Now slowly and steadily focus the magnifier on the back of your arm, the softer area. Adjust the magnifier so that the rays of sun becomes laser focused and it is red hot in that area. Be steady and keep making the focus sharper and sharper. After 30 seconds, you can stop. Open your eyes.*

By this time you must have understood the value of these experiments. Your mouth might have watered with the lemon, your heart might have been pumping with fear from the cop or your arm might have actually become hot and also burnt a little. This was a very simple experiment to prove how external reality was influenced by the inner thoughts, images and feelings.

Let me repeat this statement once more:

**Your brain cannot differentiate between
real action and mental action.**

Not only was the experiment touching on the visualization part but was also tapping into the feelings area of your heart. It is so critical a piece in your armor that in a few days or weeks from now when you go through the whole process, you will never lose an opportunity to tap into this chamber's resource for anything you would aspire anytime in your life going forward.

How does feeling bring results?

The next few paragraphs can change your life. I would suggest you read it, study it like your life depends on it. In fact it does. My life has undergone a sea change for the better applying the techniques described in this book and getting a good grasp of the power of visualization and feeling. So tighten your belts, read, understand and experiment till your conscious mind accepts them and by practice, your subconscious uses them to your benefit.

A bit of an understanding of the word quantum mechanics in lay man's language will help us here. In the physical reality, objects exist at a point in time at a particular place. In quantum mechanics, objects instead exist in a haze of probability. They have a certain chance of being in point A, another chance to be in point B and so on. It does not predict a single definite result for an observation. We do not know precisely what is going to happen in the future but rather it predicts a number of different futures, different possible outcomes and tells us how likely each of these is.

The key understanding is that the future is already created. We **choose** (mark this word!!) which of the many possibilities already created we bring to bear in our life. How do we move from one possibility to another? We can leap from one possibility to another. We can start our day in one range of possibility and through choices we make using the internal technology of visualization and feeling, we create a zone and leap from there.

Traditionally, it has always been said that we go through bad times and then enter the good time. We have been taught to assume linear progression in time. And that is the biggest fallacy that I aim to dispel. Instead of seeing things as a sequence of events, can we look into the whole point as an array of possibilities?

We embody the power to choose what we really desire to see.

The question now is : Do you know how to choose? This is the crux of this chamber's magical passage of Visualization and Feeling.

The feeling becomes the prayer. The feeling is where the birth of the possibility takes place. It is the feeling that is held close to your bosom that creates the reality for you and you become a manifestor. It is feeling *as if the prayer were already answered rather than asking that the answer come to pass.*

When your thoughts, emotions and feelings become one, you have crossed the threshold into the magical land of desires.

When you pray for something to happen, it really means that it is not here now. You tend to use the words "hope", "wish" or "try." Very well intentioned prayers do not come to fruition due to the fact we are acknowledging that what we desire is not in the present. Feel the feeling that what you desire is already there in the NOW and let your body and thoughts become one with this feeling. Thankfulness, gratitude and appreciation take the place of begging or wanting or pleading. You can call this feeling as an inner technology, an inner prayer, a belief system or anything that fits into your mental image. Let us catapult the consciousness from the non physical into the physical reality.

You have everything within you, to bring forth into reality what you intently desire.

At this point, I would ask you to pause. Breathe in deep and relax a couple of times and now go back and re-read the passage once more underlining each part that makes you think. Once you get the meaning of this passage, I can assure you the rest of the book will flow through like a gentle breeze bringing in fragrance.

Even though you are just in the second chamber, I applaud you for being in the flow thus far. If you have re-read the passage mentioned above, let us get to the action.

Action steps:

1. Enter the Alpha state as detailed in UGM Appendix A.

2. Mentally repeat the heartfelt desires one by one.

3. Take the first item on your list and visualize yourself achieving the desired object. For instance, if you desire a net increase of $50000 dollars this year over the last year, visualize the things you would do with the extra income. See your bank balance with this number. See it come alive. May be satisfy your own needs or your family needs or may be do some charity. Let this visual image touch your core being closest to the heart.

4. What do you FEEL, now that you have achieved in your inner eye. Make the feeling as intense as humanly possible. Remember: *Your brain cannot differentiate between real action and mental action.* Is it a feeling of gratitude and thankfulness that you were able to achieve? Is it a feeling of inner joy and happiness? Who are the ones closest to you to celebrate? If you are giving a small talk on this achievement, what would you say? Who is listening? Let it flow . Let it come out. If you have to emotionally let it out, please do so. There is nothing better than the Universe watching your FEELINGS in response to your achievement. To take another

example: if your list had your desire to conceive a baby, how would you feel when you discovered you are pregnant? See the soul taking the human form. See the joy, feel the joy. Go through the process. The magic is to: SEE AND FEEL AS IF IT HAS ACTUALLY HAPPENED. You are not faking it. It has triggered the process already and your inner mind can SEE it. Your heart can FEEL it. Your body transforms energetically from this act of Visualization and Feeling.

5. Repeat steps 3 and 4 for each one of your heartfelt desires. If you so choose, you can just focus on one to its complete manifestation and then pick the next. It could so happen that, just by repeating the list and visualizing and feeling only for one of them, the others get activated too. You are in for an exponential compound effect of the magic of visualization and feeling.

6. Once you are done with the above steps, get back to the Beta state by slowly mentally counting from 1 to 5, and at each number prepare yourself to come out of this active vibrant interactive session you just had. 1….2….slowly coming out….3…4….coming out now…5….Eyes wide open feeling fully refreshed knowing fully well that the magic has started happening and you know that the reality in the physical world is just round the corner.

7. Keep this sacred space you experienced this session within you only without diluting the process by scattering it to the outside world which may not see the way you have seen.

You are doing just great! Keep up the practice each and every day. By the time you are done with all the chambers, you will be introduced to the consolidated action plan that you can carry with you at all times, and in turn become an ambassador of the Manifesting Chambers.

Silence is golden we heard it many times and now it is your turn to turn your silence into gold…

MY EXPERIENCES SO FAR

Chapter 5

THE THIRD CHAMBER - THE MAGIC OF THE POWER OF SILENCE

The third chamber you are about to enter is the chamber of silence. Have you ever had a chance to experience the depth of silence? While I write this chapter, coincidentally I have been silent since the time I woke up today. One of my heartfelt desires at the beginning of the year was to have a day of silence on the fourth Saturday of every month and today is that day in the first month of the year. I do see this synchronicity of my intention to write about silence and me actually being silent for the day as a powerful force in itself to bring out the best for all those who read. It is truly magical and it is a clue to the inner mind that this is a wink from the Universe assuring me that I am on the right track. I find silence a rejuvenating, vital part of life. The world is a noisy place and as a culture we reward the loud. We leave our televisions on to keep us company. Social media and mobile phones make us feel connected to the outside world. Most of our waking state is filled with external sounds and internal chatter. Your mind has got so much habituated to these sounds that you and your mind starve for sound if you are kept isolated. Loneliness has become a curse for many. The silence could literally be deafening if you are not trained to tame the sound of silence.

What we plan to do in this chamber is not only to understand why it is so important to have the silence in our lives but also to tap into the huge manifesting power the sea of silence holds.

This calls for a small exercise before you jump forward. Read the following points first and then close your eyes for a minute to do the steps:

- Take a deep breath in and let it out, relaxing your whole body and repeat it twice.
- Put the intention out to the Universe: "I am ready to get trained to use the power of silence to manifest my heartfelt desires."
- Watch your breath flowing in and going out. Any thoughts that might come during this minute, gently say in silence "Thank you. I am in training". Mentally put a "Do not disturb" board outside the gates of your thinking mind.
- After a minute, heave a sigh of relief and say out aloud with a positive frame of mind and voice: "Wow, I can do this. I think I can!"

Meaning of being silent

Silence provides a space for reflection and contemplation. Intentional silence allows you to watch your patterns. Quietude is something you have to consciously cultivate. Literally, you can make silence a slice of heaven. As you master this art of silence, you would thirst for the peace and recharging that comes from even a small session of silence.

Silence is the gap that exists between your habitual thoughts. It is estimated that an average adult has around 30000 to 50000 thoughts a day and most of them are patterned and habitual. We are already in that continuum where there are sounds, thoughts and chatter on either side of the gaps. The lesser the gap, the more the chaos, the lesser the clarity. It is like a glass of muddy water. Keep stirring the water and the water will stay muddy. Let the glass stand silently and you see the water getting clearer by the minute.

The same principle applies to your mind. You need to make it silent for the power of clarity, the power of focus and the most important of all; the power to manifest. Silence is not the absence of something but the presence of everything.

Creation in the gap

It is in the gaps or in the silence that creation takes place. It is the gaps that holds the Universe together and it is here where the limitless possibilities we discussed in the previous chamber come into play and you become the co-creator. In fact, what we humans consider as silence, in the cosmos it is literally vibrating and pulsating with energy in a myriad network of countless complex structures that is continuously working with our thoughts, feelings and actions. Even though we don't need a proof of science here, nevertheless for the scientific mind, a lot of research has gone through on how the universe constantly keeps vibrating with energy. Higgs Boson or the particle mind conducted at CERN is one such phenomenon that has been termed as a manifestation model.

Creation needs space or a gap. The gap or this space is the place that allows us to build, create and manifest. When we tap into the silence, we make conscious contact with the all-powerful Universe (aka Super Power or Higher Consciousness or God), the source of all energy. It is here in the silence that we realign our intentions to the creative energy.

> *It's a silence that has a lot of activity. ...Gary Busey*

Entering the silence

Entering the silence is a technique that can be mastered with dedicated practice. The technique can be used anywhere, anytime (except when you are driving of course). But it is recommended you do this as a part of your daily morning and/or evening routine. Again, be cautious not to let any of the techniques become a chore or a mechanical part of your day. Each time you sit and begin the process, keep a child like curiosity that will help you to have new experiences and would hasten the process of manifestation. Remember, the equation works with mathematical precision. Your job is to get to the end of the solution with the steps clearly laid out.

All creation has a foundation in silence.

Action steps:

1. Enter the Alpha state by following the UGM Appendix A. This step with little practice should take you about 2 minutes.

2. Mentally slowly repeat the heartfelt desires one by one.

3. Take a deep breath (inhale to a count of 4) through your nostrils and exhale as if it is coming out from the center of your forehead between your eyebrows (around an inch inside). The exhalation should be so slow that if you placed a candle flame near your nostril, that flame should hardly flicker with the outgoing breath. If you run out of the outgoing breath, you can take the next inhalation and follow the same pattern. It is normal to feel a sensation or vibration at the center of your forehead. Repeat this step 3 times.

4. Let's take one step higher. Do not at any time strain your breath or make yourself uncomfortable. It gets easier with each passing breath and each passing day. Visualize for a few seconds at the center of your forehead, the first of your desires (you can keep a priority of your list that you can follow each time you take this step). Take a deep breath (to a count of 4) and during exhalation create a gap between your lower and upper lips and say out loud the word " AAHHHHHHH …." in a continuous flow to a count of 10. While this vibration is being created, let your awareness travel from the base of your spine all the way up to the center of your forehead. You are in the silence and creating the vibration with

the sound of "AAHHHHHHH ..." that does not allow any external sound or your internal thoughts to penetrate.

5. Take a deep breath (inhale to a count of 4) and while exhaling, create a gap between your lower and upper lips and repeat the word "AAHHHHHHH...in a continuous flow to a count of 10 that would travel from the center of your forehead all the way through your spine to the base of your spine. Imagine the object of your desire being delivered.

6. Step 4 and 5 make up one round. Repeat the steps 4 and 5 for each item in your list to a total of 4 rounds. So it is 4 inhalations and 4 exhalations. I have found 4 breaths to be optimal to trigger the depth of silence.

For instance, if one of your desires was to increase your income by $50000 dollars this year, you would visualize money bundles or money's worth at the center of your forehead in step 4, and in step 5, you would see the money being delivered by your out breath at the end of the spine. This could be money, your new car, your baby, your new job or any of them on your list that you had created in Chapter 2.

My own example might be a case in point. I had started working on this chamber around 8 years ago. My curiosity resulted in trying to prove to myself that this technique works.

You are always welcome to test out things from an openness of mind than to begin the test with an element of doubt.

I set an intention that I am a money magnet and that money would flow to me. After all , money is energy, so I intended to manifest this energy by my own energy space. After a few days of me doing this technique, I was walking on the street of New York when I found a dollar note literally flying in the air and landing right in front of me for me to pick up. I took the dollar note and shouted from within ; "I am a money magnet. Thank you. Thank you." and thanked the Universe for manifesting my desire so quickly. Such occurrences have become very common. I continued the practice each day and a few days later, while entering a pizza place with my family, I found strewn across the corridor 5 , 10 and 20 dollar notes. Anyone who would have passed that area even 10 seconds earlier would have got it. How come I was there at the right time to pick up those notes in excitement and thanking the Universe again. Such instances have been very frequent since then resulting in two big glass jars filled to the brim with coins and currency notes from different countries. I have been able to manifest health and total cure from a non-curable (according to the doctors) illness just with this technique along with what I discussed in the previous chapter. I have manifested a well paying job from a spam email that for no apparent reason I happened to check. I am in awe each time I do. I have come out of testing phase a long time back and now I know, given the right intention with a good dose of belief and a set of techniques, one can achieve anything. You can learn more about what this can do in www.ultimateguidetomanifestation.com.

A small side note for those who start manifesting money this way. Do not spend the money on yourself or give it away to charity, but store them in a jar that is visible to you in a prominent place in your house. It is always a reminder of the power of silence and that the magical manifestation can always be worked to your benefit and in turn to the benefit of your fellow human beings. With this technique, you would find opportunities from the network of silence open up, that would allow you to earn and enjoy the benefits.

You attract what you deserve by what you become and not what you want.

I am as excited as you are now and am rearing to get to the next chamber to churn the ether with magical vibrations.

MY EXPERIENCES SO FAR

Chapter 6

THE FOURTH CHAMBER - THE MAGIC OF VIBRATIONS LEVEL 1 and 2

Welcome to the magic of vibrations. This chamber will challenge your ego. You will be introduced to powerful vibrations to speed up your manifestation process. Even though you might have already started seeing results using the magic of the previous chambers, the techniques in this chamber will propel you further and you will observe yourself surrounded by the energies of the objects of your desires. In a way you have already been exposed to the power to some extent by the sound of "AAHHHHH..." I believe you have experimented with the technique in the last chapter and you would have experienced the whole body vibrating with energy.

You are almost half way to manifesting your heart's desires and some of you who have already started the practice in right earnest might have already been experiencing noticeable changes to your mental appetite. You have already rehearsed your desire list multiple times and your inner visual imagery is building up with solid foundation.

At this stage, I would encourage you to create a vision board with concrete believable pictures related to your core desires. You can find a good example of a vision board in www.ultimateguideto manifestation.com. There is more clarity at this point in your manifesting career so to speak. The vision board will bring to life with deeper conviction that you are on the right track. To a large extent you are seeing light at the end of the proverbial tunnel. Take time to create the vision list that satisfies your heart.

It amazes me as to the synchronicities that take place, when the intention is set with a true desire to serve others. My intention for this chapter was to provide you with 2 powerful vibrations that would become a sacred space within your pursuit of your desires, wherein realities magically appear. And these vibrations have everything to do with the mixture of the Vedic and the Egyptian vibrations for wealth and anything you desire intently from the heart. These are powerful vibratory words that I will be explaining shortly. While I am writing this chapter, working on the flow of my thoughts, I turned my attention for a brief minute to an advertisement that appeared on the TV and I hear a movie called "Gods of Egypt" to be released in a few weeks. I have no idea what the movie is supposed to deliver but with certainty and a knowing I can tell that, it was a wink from the Universe that approved this chapter and the message intended to deliver.

I encourage you to notice such encounters in your daily life, and make a note in a journal. Each such event triggers another set of events, and you become a point of contact for the Universe to weave the magic for your own desires and also for others who are intently seeking to better their lives.

How does vibration play out?

You are not a physical being in a physical universe. You are a spiritual, vibrational being in a vibrational universe. Manifestation occurs when the energy of your intentional desires matches the vibrations that you create within your inner space. The Universe is in a constant state of receiving signals from your consciousness. It is an equation that you have to work out. One side of that equation is already set and you need to match it on the other side with your vibrations. The Universe rewards consistency and persistency of these vibrations you emit.

At this point, you are already coming to accept that your vibrational self attracts the vibrational blueprint of the object you desire. Remember, you can always turn on the vibrational switch to be in your favor. If you are an over achiever already, great!! See if you have attained your desires in all areas that we are working with in this book. Each item on your list has a different frequency and thus a different vibration. You do not need to understand what that frequency is. That is the work of this chamber. It has nothing do with any of the faiths that you sometimes believe it to be. The magic of vibrations occurs when you follow the steps laid out and tune into the Universe through these two powerful sounds in a step by step approach.

Let me caution you that your ego could be challenged, and you need to be aware of the small inner voice that will grab this opportunity to move you towards known old habits and beliefs as you move through unchartered waters.

As mentioned before, do not put your energy on those inner disempowering voices, instead try out these time tested ways to keep the ego at bay. Mentally say; "Thank you for sharing." You may also repeat internally; "I know that I am manifesting my heartfelt desires that would benefit me and the lives of many whom I get an opportunity to impact positively." I encourage you to set aside all judgments and let your body, mind and your entire inner space be vibrating with the sounds of the following vibrations.

The meaning attached to these sounds is a bit arbitrary, as there cannot be any real intelligent way of explaining a vibration except that the usage of this sound needs to be experienced. What I have presented below is a very close effect of what you could experience after practicing them for a few days or weeks.

Vibration Level 1 - The sound of RAA and LAASUNKAAN

RAA (pronounced RAAA-AAAH for ten seconds) is the element of fire within you that propels you to intensely seek out your desires. It is the vibratory power of Sun that burns out anything in the way of your progress. There is no literal meaning to this sound other than being a vibration. When repeated over and over again, this sound creates a laser focus similar to the magnifying glass and it is this focus that brings together people, objects, circumstances that aid you in your progress. You will observe that, with constant practice this sound merges with the sound of "AAAHHHH" introduced earlier.

LAASUNKAAN (pronounced LAAAH-SOON-KAAAN) is the energy of wealth that is not limited to money. Wealth is always a much larger vibration that includes the energy of happiness, money, relationship, spirituality and health. In other words, when you manifest a major portion of your desires you started this book with, you are wealthy beyond imagination. This vibratory power has its source in ancient Egypt.

Action Steps:

1. Enter the Alpha state by following the UGM Appendix A.
2. Mentally repeat slowly the heartfelt desires one by one.
3. Put your awareness at the Solar Plexus (just behind the navel area).
4. Repeat the word "RAAAAH" and alternate with the word "LAASUNKAAN." Feel the intense vibration at the Solar Plexus area. Let the word come out of your mouth loud and clear. Let each word be coming out for as long as you physically can. 5 to 10 seconds for each word is excellent. Your vibration will not only impact you in an energetic, positive way but also your whole household or community is impacted. The key is to focus in the area and feel the vibrations. Repeat this step at least 9 times before moving on to the next vibrational level described below.

"If you want to find the secrets of the universe, think in terms of energy, frequency and vibration."—Nikola Tesla

Vibration Level 2- The sound of KHEPERUS'AUNGKH

KHEPERUS'AUNGKH (pronounced KHAY-PAY-ROOS-AUNKH) is the energy of life force given to the desire to bring into existence. You are training your mind to use the power of this vibration to attract like a magnet. You create an environment that creates a pull, and once the energies of the objects get sucked into your being, it is magical to see it happen in the physical world. This vibration has been well known in the ancient Egyptian culture to bring forth into reality anything the mind can perceive and believe. We will be using a visualization process to capture the vibration in your being and for that purpose, we use the following two images. This image is called the Eye of Horus or the Eye of RAAA or the all seeing Eye.

The other image we use is of the cosmic dust along with a spiral of galaxies.

Action Steps:

1. Enter the Alpha state by following the UGM Appendix A.
2. Mentally repeat slowly the heartfelt desires one by one.
3. Imagine the famous "Eye" in the center of your chest and place the desire in the black spot of the "Eye".
4. Imagine yourself in deep deep space and feel the energy of the space spin in your heart in a clockwise direction. You might start feeling a tiny flame providing you warmth.
5. Feel the spin moving faster and faster like a whirlwind. Let it accelerate.
6. Feel the cosmic dust particles in its bright golden color gravitate towards you and spinning.
7. Feel the color of Red and then Blue and finally White spinning around you with brighter and brighter intensity like an explosion.
8. Feel yourself at the center of your own giant Sun, your own star. The black dot of the "Eye" attracts like a black hole in the Universe everything what you have intensely desired.
9. See in your mind's eye explosion all around you. These are your new points, new possibilities that bring to reality the people, books, activities, opportunities to help you manifest.
10. See each one of your desires entering the "Eye" into your heart.
11. Now let the vibration of "KHEPERUS-AUNGKH" come out loud and clear from your vocal chords. Repeat this vibrational sound a minimum of 9 times (as you keep practicing, you tend to increase this number that is highly beneficial to fulfillment of your dreams).

This vibration implies creation coming to life from nothingness. The energies are created between the manifest and the un-manifest and a dynamic energetic bridge created for the desires to come to reality. It also means that, even if you do not have the resources to manifest or back you up, you do have the power of the Universe to help you from the depth of the cosmic matter. You are creating a new world, a new dream with the power of your mind and the vibrations of this sound.

Pat yourself on your back, go out into the open and shout at the top of your lungs to the infinite sky above you during a starry night. Do something that will burst your inner joy and feelings of what you have accomplished so far going through these magical chambers. I promise it is going to be a smooth ride onward. You have come thus far proving to yourself that you were meant to do and be someone greater than what you thought. Your attitude would have turned upward with a very strong foundation of belief. You are humble enough to move forward and be in the realm of vibrations and feelings.

I applaud you for going through this chamber that might have challenged you to some extent. Keep rocking and keep churning the ether. It is your life, your dreams and your desires.

You are now about to enter the realm of your Quantum influence where you meet your alternate Self. I am so excited to introduce you to your perfect YOU.

There is as much in that little space within the heart as there is in the whole world outside. Heaven, earth, fire, wind, sun, moon, lightning, stars; whatever is and whatever is not, everything is there."Upanishad"

Suresh Harvu

MY EXPERIENCES SO FAR

Chapter 7

THE FIFTH CHAMBER - THE MAGIC OF UNIVERSAL QUANTUM INFLUENCE

You are not alone in this process of manifesting your heart's desires. Even though the list is yours, you have with you limitless help coming to your aid. You have already encountered the wonderful Energy packets through the vibrational power of silence and the vibrational power of words. We will embark upon a journey to tap into the unlimited potential that exists at multiple levels at the same time.

Dream is not that which you see while sleeping, it is something that does not let you sleep --APJ Abdul Kalam

When we talk about multiple things happening at the same time in different places, we refer to that as quantum. Quantum is a field of potentialities. What this means is there is more than one result waiting to happen in a whole array of possibilities. Heisenberg the physicist said. "When we observe something, both the observer and the observed are changed." You get to change everything by the way you look at it with the intention behind it.

This chapter explores in a very practical way the usage of this Quantum Influence in the pursuit of your goals and dreams. It is all about the influence you are surrounded with. Without your permission, you have been influenced to a large extent by your parents, teachers, society and the economy. Your present circumstances are proof enough of this fact unless you consciously attempt to take control of your thoughts, intentions, feelings and are armed with tools that assist you in getting out of the herd mentality.

You have come a long way so far through these chambers that are already influencing you to greater heights. You have already started to become a magnetic personality creating a shield around you that screens the vibrations that are being created every single moment of your life. You have made the decision to change for the better. Your past is not equal to your future. You are not waiting for things to happen; instead the Universe is waiting for your demands. Do you feel this way? Are you getting that powerful surge inside of you?

I have always been drawn towards people, books, jobs, and seminars that have always been an eye opener. I have a knowing that I am being led from one level to the next level in the pursuit of understanding life itself. I have used the techniques of this chamber to create a wonderful, powerful visualization process with a clear objective to be achieved. The results that I get in guiding others with these have been nothing short of magical. Results include better and more satisfying jobs, better health, and better, improved relationships, to name a few. I have distilled the complex methods and concepts of Quantum approaches into the following two parts, each one can be used by itself to transform your life. As both of them relate to infinite possibilities, they are grouped under the Quantum Influence.

Universal Quantum Influence

- The doorway to the other side for Universal help
- The doorway to meeting your alternate Self

The doorway to the other side for Universal help

This is the other side that is the source of the world, where your vibrations are being put together to bring forth creation of your desires, and you become the co-creator with the Universe. Visible proof is always the result of the process in the invisible realm. You always have help on the other side that can be used to your advantage. It is a good idea at this stage to highlight a few universal laws that have been designed for your benefit.

Every thought, feeling and action has an entry into the metaphysical bank balance. Build up a sizable inventory of positive, empowering thoughts that you can constantly add to your metaphysical bank balance. Each time you think a good thought, your balance increases. Each time you do the action steps of these chambers, your balance increases. You can always draw upon this balance to satisfy your need. You earned it and you are entitled to spend it.

Everything is on a continuum and has an opposite. We can suppress and transform undesirable thoughts by concentrating on the opposite pole. Higher vibrations consume and transform lower ones; thus, each of us can change the energies in our lives by understanding the law of vibrations.

> ***If you can see it in your mind you will hold it in your hand***
> ***- Bob Proctor***

You will now put on your visualization cap and be ready to take the journey to the other side. That is the area of sub conscious or super conscious or Universal consciousness, whatever way you can label them. The other side is the side of higher vibrations; a no-limit zone on the highway to accelerated achievement. Keep your visit to the other side only to yourself. This ensures laser focus effort that would bring forth magical realities. Once you manifest your reality, you will be called upon to come to the aid of your fellow beings. As suggested earlier, having a journal is a good idea to capture your experiences and your thoughts.

Action Steps:

Read the following steps, absorbing the intent behind them and then close your eyes and go through the process. You will need to read this each time you start the process and it takes a week to do this on your own.

1. Enter the Alpha state.
2. Pick one of the desires from your list and mentally affirm it with total belief.
3. Imagine a closed golden doorway 6 feet in front of you enveloped in a radiant white light that separates the visible from the invisible creative source. Feel the brilliance of the light.
4. Slowly walk towards the door knowing that it will open.
5. As you approach the door, it opens to a beautiful staircase with 9 steps leading down. You are starting to climb down slowly one step at a time while counting backwards in your mind from 9 to 1. The whole area below is strewn with fresh rose petals on a velvet like grass with an aroma from the blossoms. There is a golden key lying on the petals that you pick up.
6. Keep walking wherever the path takes you and you arrive at a beautifully decked building, the Universal Help Building. All are welcome into this building. Open the door with the golden key and enter the building with measured steps. The ceiling is high, beautifully decorated and at the center of the big hall is a white marble platform on which to sit. There is a life size mirror exactly in front of the platform. Go ahead and sit and relax on the marble stone. Take a nice deep breath.
7. Look into the mirror and ask the image to show the fulfillment of your desires. Now be patient and silent and watch the unfolding in the mirror.
8. Watch the YOU in the mirror getting transformed into the person you believe yourself to be. The object of your desire is right in front of you. See yourself accomplishing. See yourself holding the object. See yourself feeling the joy of achieving. Nothing stands

in your way. See that car you desire, the house you wish to live in, the job that you were waiting for, the bundle of currency notes you hold, the soul mate you secretly nurtured, see yourself in perfect health with the size you wished, the weight you have always hoped to reach, and see yourself totally rid of any health issues you were facing. You are seeing it all. Be in the moment. Feel the peace and joy of accomplishment. You have the golden key in your hand to unlock your potential.
9. Sit for as long as you would like to. When you are done, gently get up from the marble platform, look at the ceiling with a sense of gratitude and happiness and affirm silently "I am the person in the mirror. I have accomplished all my heart's desires" and then start walking back the way you came. The door to the Universal Help building automatically closes behind you. You have the key and you can go there anytime you wish.
10. As you walk back along the path filled with rose petals, feel the warmth of accomplishment. Leave the golden key on any of the petals and slowly start climbing the 9 steps and come out into your world while the golden door closes behind you.

Mentally count very slowly from 1 to 5 and on the count of 5, open your eyes, wide awake, fully refreshed knowing that you were on the other side and that you have put in motion all things that are needed for your desires to come true.

Let me ask you a question and you can answer it to yourself or to any other person who is supporting you in your endeavor. How are you feeling now? How eager are you now to get going with the process?

The doorway to meeting your alternate Self

This method is a variation of the one described above in that you are now guided to go into the outer space to meet your perfect YOU (Self) who is perfect in all aspects and has all that you intend to have. If your intention was to manifest money or write a book or become an artist or have your own successful business or be cured of a health issue that has been termed as incurable, this alternate self of yours has already achieved it.

You tap into the unseen power of this Self and get your questions answered and all your desires fulfilled. It is as simple as that. Of course, it takes consistent practice to remove all the disbelief and self doubts. As I repeatedly mention throughout this book the Universe matches your vibrations to provide you more than you ask for.

When you meet your perfect Self, you start cloning all the attributes of that other Self and carry with you the vibrational blueprint required to become the co-creator of your desires.

> ***The subconscious mind is aware of the many worlds unfolding in each moment.--Kevin Michel***

Find a suitable place to be undisturbed for a period of 10 minutes. The longer you stay the better. My calculation is simple. Take your current age and spend that many minutes doing these exercises in these chambers. You will later be provided with a plan of action that you can do in these number of minutes. So for example, if you are 25 years old, you invest a minimum of 25 minutes of your day.

Action Steps:

Read the following steps absorbing the intent behind it and then close your eyes and go through the process. You will need to read this each time you start the process and it takes a week to do this on your own.

1. Enter the Alpha state.
2. Pick one of the desires from your list and mentally affirm it with total belief.
3. Imagine a hall way at the bottom of 9 steps and start climbing

down slowly from a count of 9 to 1. Nine...Eight..Seven.. Six..Five..Four..Three..Two..One. After the last step you step into the hallway.
4. Six feet in front of you, you see a large beautifully carved, golden colored double door.
5. On the other side of the door is the infinite Universe in the infinity of time with infinite possibilities and parallel Universes floating around.
6. You start walking towards the door fully enveloped in white light, ready to meet your perfect Self. In a count of 1...2...3, the doors are wide open and you step out.
7. You are now in a sea of limitless vibrations. The light around you starts gathering the vibrations. You are surrounded by a whirlwind of golden cosmic dust, each particle representing parallel Universes and in the midst of them, you meet your perfect Self. Be an observer for some time.
8. You see your other Self exactly the way you imagined yourself to be, the perfect person with perfect health having perfect relationships with plenty of wealth and all the talents required for a perfect journey of your life. Hold hands with your other Self and let the vibrational blue print transfer to you that is needed for your manifestation. Let yourself dance to the tune of the cosmic vibration.
9. Stay there for as long as you feel like, and then on a mental count of 1 to 3, come back to the place from where you started.

The doors close behind you after you enter. You now have met and acquired all that you ever need to take the next steps.

You have just completed an advanced manifestation technique through this chamber. If it appears simple, just master the steps. If it appears too complex for your mind in training, spend more time on each chamber before proceeding. I have found that a week is a good time to start and grasp the process well.

You have a heart's desire to make your dreams come true. You have taken up the challenge and you are blazing through. You are within reach to the finish line. Continue being your true self and let the next chamber lift you to the highest level.

Your caravan is moving on.

MY EXPERIENCES SO FAR

Chapter 8

THE SIXTH CHAMBER - THE MAGIC OF THE POWER OF I AM THAT I AM

Congratulations!! You have put yourself way ahead of the crowd. You have already started taking measurable action steps in the previous chambers. Some of them might have been relatively easier than others. Success need not become a complex task. Your brain neural networks have begun their shift. You might have also experienced synchronicities that are making some sense to you. You have started to connect the dots.

This chamber is probably the easiest to go through as far as instructions are concerned. But I have found the magic of this chamber to far exceed my expectations. Before I go ahead with this magical power, let us do a small checkpoint of your progress.

With all sincerity to the purpose of your heart's inherent desires and you following the steps laid out so far in this book, rate yourself from a scale of 1 to 10 (a 10 indicating *absolutely true* and a 1 indicating that you have *still to catch up*) to the following questions. The number that first comes to your mind on reading the statement is the one you write. Use a pencil to write the responses so that you can go back again at a later stage to refine your answers.

a. I have the **LIST** of my heart's desires clearly outlined and do not need to refer to it each time I practice the action steps.
b. I do **BELIEVE** that I can achieve all my heart's desires within a very short span of time of 2 to 5 years (some of them in a few weeks/months).

c. I have a very clear **INTENTION** to achieve the desires for my own benefit and for the benefit of others, and that I put the intention out to the Universe each time I practice.
d. I am able to **VISUALIZE** clearly the object of my desire each time I practice.
e. I develop a very strong **FEELING**, sometimes filled with emotion of having visualized myself achieving.
f. I can feel the **SILENCE** between my thoughts and know that the silence is where the creation is.
g. I feel the **VIBRATIONS** of the words I have started to use and know that consistent usage of those words creates a dynamic field of attraction.
h. I am able to touch the **SOURCE** on the other side and come back, fully aware of the fact that I am empowered by my other Self.
i. I am ready to witness the **MAGIC** happening all around me, and I know that I am responsible for the creation in my life going forward. I know that the future is being created in the present through my **THOUGHTS**.

Change is the only constant in this journey and you will have observed that you have come a far way from where you began. Check-pointing is a good way for you to go back to those chambers and repeat them until your inner mind accepts the invisible reality.

THE POWER OF 5 WORDS "I AM THAT I AM"

It is said that a man is known by the company he seeks and the words he uses. Your practice of the action steps so far in this book would mean that, you have kept an excellent company with your thought process and the vibration you are creating in the pursuit of manifestation. You in turn would attract the right people and all the right circumstances, and you with an open heart would be welcoming them in your space.

Similarly, the words you speak have their origin in your thoughts. Words have power, as we have seen in the previous chambers. What I am introducing here is 5 magical, powerful words that continue your quest for increasing your vibrational quotient, seals the process of manifestation and opens you up at the perfect time for you to harvest the results.

As mentioned before, you can either give a meaning to these words or you can start using the vibrations of these words to your benefit. I would encourage the readers to suspend any disempowering thoughts or judgments that can stray you from the path of achieving your heart's desires.

There has never been a statue erected to honor a critic. --Zig Ziglar

I wish upon you to build statues inside of you of your towering accomplishments, however small or big they seem to be. Let the small voices drown in the ocean of your vibrational blueprint you are carrying at all times.
Let the following words soak your mind each day as you continue your quest for manifesting your heart's desires.

Action steps:

a. Enter the Alpha state.
b. Use a full minute to repeat these words very slowly in your inner mind for 9 times(each taking about 6 seconds) - I AM THAT I AM... I AM THAT I AM ..I AM THAT I AM ..I AM THAT IAM ..I AM THAT I AM..I AM THAT I AM..I AM THAT I AM..I AM THAT I AM..I AM THAT I AM
c. For the next 2 minutes, start internalizing the following words. Repeat them very slowly, feeling the feeling that comes along with these words. For instance, in the words : I AM LIGHT... visualize and feel the light enveloping you for the duration of the word.

I AM LOVE – feel the love pouring from your heart
I AM LIGHT – feel yourself enveloped by the healing light
I AM BLISS – feel the moment of pure joy
I AM HEALTH – feel your body vibrant
I AM LOVE – feel the love pouring from your heart
I AM VITALITY – feel the vibrance in your body
I AM ENERGY – feel the tingling sensations in your body
I AM LOVE ENERGY – feel the love energy surrounding you
I AM LIGHT ENERGY – feel the soft healing light surrounding you
I AM HEALTH ENERGY – feel the vibrance in every cell of your body
I AM PEACE – feel the calmness in your breath
I AM LOVE – feel the love pouring from your heart
I AM FORGIVING – feel the freedom of forgiving
I AM RECEIVING – feel the abundance coming to you
I AM MANIFESTING – feel the power of creativity
I AM THE FLOW – feel the continuity like a flowing stream
I AM MAGNETIC – feel the attraction in your spine
I AM MAJESTIC – feel the magnificence of the Universe inside you
I AM HAPPY – feel the joy permeating you
I AM DIVINE – feel the power of your spiritual Self
I AM THAT I AM – feel one with your Creator the Universal Mind
(Repeat it a few times)

Come out of this state with a count of 1 to 5. 1…2…3 (slowly coming out of the state)..4..5. You are wide awake feeling energized and one with the Universal vibration.

The power of these words, when internalized on a daily basis shifts your consciousness level up, leading you on the path of eternal progress. Your list from where you started this journey is just a fraction of what you can achieve in this journey called Life.

As you get to terms with knowing your inner core strength and see it manifest in front of your eyes, you will be resetting your vibrational thermostat to a level where manifestation and synchronicities would become a regular phenomenon. David Hawkins, in his book "Power Vs Force," has provided a very detailed practical explanation and application of calibration of one's consciousness.

I encourage you to make the words mentioned above a mantra for yourself, and when used with the sea of vibrations you created in the earlier chapters, you are very close to becoming the person that you truly were intended to be.

"You provided me the blueprint my dear traveler and I am doing my action part on the other side and I am providing you opportunities to take action...I am waiting...." --The Universe

Suresh Harvu

MY EXPERIENCES SO FAR

Chapter 9

THE SEVENTH CHAMBER - THE MAGIC OF POSITIVE ACTION

Applied knowledge is power.

Before you understand what action is being referred to here, let me summarize what it takes to manifest anything you sincerely and intently desire.

Repetition is the mother of skill. --Tony Robbins

a. **Desires** - You built up a small list of desires that you would like to manifest in the next 1 to 2 years
b. **Belief** - With positive affirmations and changing the way you nurture your desires, you started to build up belief that you can achieve.
c. **Intention** - You start creating powerful flow of thoughts through the intentions you put out into the invisible Universe. You have started the creation of new neural patterns in your brain.
d. **Visualize** - If you can believe it and see it in your inner eye, you create it. Through consistent disciplined practice you reach a stage when you can vividly see the end result.
e. **Feelings** - The Universe has started its work with the vibrations you emit, the way you feel. There is no distinction for the mind between real and unreal, and if you can feel it, you have set the process in motion.
f. **Silence** - All creation comes out of nothingness. There is power in the silence, in the gaps between thoughts. The longer the gaps,

the more room you create for manifestation. You have started using the sound of creation "**AAAAHH**" in the gaps that allows no thoughts to permeate and that your intentions take roots.

g. **Words** – Words that you speak have power to create powerful vibrations. These words (LAASUNKAAAN, RAAA, KHEPERUS'AUNGKH) increases exponentially the speed of manifestation. You give tremendous thrust to the process of creation and you have literally shortened the time it takes to see your desires in your physical Universe.

h. **Your perfect Self** - There is always a perfect Self of yours on the other side. Your alternate Self is already in possession of all that you have thought of and are striving to achieve. You draw the power and belief by going over to the other side using the Quantum mindset and coming back with a knowing that you have what it takes to cross the finish line.

i. **I AM THAT I AM** - Gratitude takes the highest place, and you are now consciously aware of the power of I AM. After the words I AM, your brain is now wired to use words that empower, uplift and strengthen you. Fear and gratitude cannot occupy the same space. You build up an arsenal where no outside negative forces can ever penetrate.

I would recommend you write down the main bullet points of the I AMs on an index card and keep it with you at all times and look at it once a day. You will be mastering the list and each day when you get ready to take action, you will be on a roll.

You can also go to my website www.ultimateguidetomanifestation.com and look for the list and print it out. You are now ready for action in the outer world and to be a part of the minority of people who make things happen instead of waiting for things to happen or wondering why things happened.

There is nothing out of the ordinary that you need to do. It is the way your mind has been trained so far that makes a difference in the way

The Ultimate Guide to Manifestation

your action gets recognized. The following actions steps will be in addition to the internal actions you have taken so far.

Action Steps:

1. Set up a game plan - This is the most important action step you will be taking in the home stretch of the manifesting process.

Take your journal out and write down the list that you started in chapter 1 in the following manner and under each of them write your goal or desire, what you need to give up in order to manifest, the rewards you get and the action you need to take.

Also more importantly, write down the possible help you expect to receive from the Universe. Let the Universe provide for you the way it knows best, but writing it down will let your consciousness be aware of the various possibilities.

Let me give an example (most of them are my real life scenarios) under each of them to demonstrate the game plan. Your goal is to write them down based on your list. (See chart on pages 78 and 79.)

2. Open yourself to ALL *insignificant events* in your day to day life.

3. Look for synchronicities that appear to be fluke or an accident. Carl Jung explains: Events are "meaningful coincidences" if they occur with no causal relationship, yet seem to be meaningfully related.

4. Align your actions with your blueprint that you created in the previous chambers. If you see or feel that the actions are not in sync with your vibrational energies you are creating every day, then follow the energy pattern.

	GOAL	WHAT TO GIVE UP	REWARD	ACTION	UNIVERSE HELP
SPIRITUAL	I AM waking up at 5 am every day to meditate	Some sleep time and some comfort	Create a new habit	Pick good books from library. Plan to sleep by 10:30 PM and set alarm to wake up by 5 AM.	You might receive a flyer for a meditation event. You are asked to coach someone at 5 am. You might wake up at 5 AM by outside sounds. **These are winks from Universe. Take action right away. Listen from your heart!!**
FAMILY	Planning vacation with family and making it fun.	Some money and days off from work.	Stress free time with loved ones and rejuvenation.	Implement the JARS (check website for details) to build up funds for the trip. Google exotic vacation spots at a reasonable distance and price. Plan days off at work in advance. Book vacation rooms in advance to get discounts. Visualize each night the fun you have on these vacations.	Unexpected bonus at work for good performance. You are assigned a role in the same location as you had planned your vacation. You see pictures of the vacation spots in local magazines. **These are winks from Universe. Take action right away. Listen from your heart!!**
HEALTH	Get rid of an existing health issue. Get into shape.	Give up complaining or discussing about the issue. Change food habits eg: give up coffee, become a vegetarian.	Better health. Manage or get rid of pain. Total freedom from chronic health issue.	Read positive healing affirmations each and every day (visit website for list of affirmations). Seek alternate healing methods (contact author for Energy Healing options). Intensify visualization and vibrational methods. Encourage others with similar issue and uplift their morale.	A book dealing with same health issue shows up. An old acquaintance may cross your path and provide you information about a healing system. You may wake up one day without any pain. A new drug invented for exactly the same issue. A chance encounter with a stranger who becomes your health coach. **These are winks from Universe. Take action right away. Listen from your heart!!**

The Ultimate Guide to Manifestation

FINANCE	Have 3 sources of income.	Give up listening to naysayers who cannot think on the lines of your new thought patterns. Change perception of rich and famous and see them as someone who have achieved through persistence and perseverance.	Financial Freedom. Money chasing you. Getting out of debt (GOOD)	Read books about creating wealth. Be open to look at ALL opportunities that knock on your door. Bring up old desires and talents and work on them. Be willing to take knowledgeable and reasonable risk.	A free ticket to an educational seminar that teaches you multiple sources of income generation. You meet a stranger and become good friends and you are introduced to a business opportunity. An offer to do a part time job. You find a brochure in your mailbox regarding income generation. **These are winks from Universe. Take action right away. Listen from your heart!!**
CAREER	Get out of mechanical job life and do what you are passionate about.	Comfort of having a pay check. Not willing to make changes for betterment.	Living life to the fullest with passion. Financial Freedom. Choices in Life.	Take lessons on your existing skills. Start a free course in the area of your passion and offer to friends and families. Search for jobs that provide more free time. Become a voracious reader of books on the subject of your passion.	An unexpected call from a company with availability for a position. You are asked to help out an organization on weekends and you meet a person who gives you an idea. You are transferred to another department that gives more flexible work schedules. **These are winks from Universe. Take action right away. Listen from your heart!!**

5. Draw a line and start fresh in your manifestation process, if you find yourself out of touch with the process. You will do a discredit to all your efforts that you have already put in by bringing in an energy of regret.

Regret is the greatest stumbling block in a person's journey in life.

I am so thrilled with your progress. You have traveled the path laid out and have put yourself in the drivers seat of consciously manifesting your heart's desires. You are unstoppable going forward. Keep up the good work and continue moving forward for a short span of time to crystallize your dreams and goals list and make it a physical reality.

MY EXPERIENCES SO FAR

Chapter 10

THE EIGHTH CHAMBER - THE MAGIC OF 40 DAY CHUNKING

Yes!!! You can feel it. You have seen it throughout this book. You have practiced it each and every day, and if you have missed, there are no regrets and you continue building up on the foundation you have laid.

It is now time to draw up a MAP (Massive Action Plan) for exactly one year. If you have already started practicing daily the action steps laid out in each and every chapter, I would venture to say that you are an achiever, a success in your own right and results would have shown up in your external world. You always build up on the previous victories however small or insignificant they may be.

Significance of 40

There is some level of importance to the number 40 in most of the world cultures. I have found substantial explanation to the number 40 that inspired me to create a plan of 40 days for achieving anything big in your life. Just a few notes might be of interest to the reader:
The Hebrew people lived in the Sinai desert for "forty years."
Jesus fasted "forty days and forty nights" in the Judean desert.
Muhammad was forty years old when he first received the revelation delivered by the archangel Gabriel.
In Hinduism, some popular religious prayers consist of forty shlokas or dohas (couplets, stanzas).
Some of the popular fasting period last 40 days.
A full term of pregnancy lasts for 40 weeks.

40 Day Chunking

I have observed that 40 day chunks (or blocks) hold a good time period for training oneself and seeing movement in the physical world, that shows clear signs that you are on the path to self discovery and achievement. When you follow the 40 day method, you get 9 such cycles of time in a year (40 * 9=360). I like to see movement in all of your categories that you started this journey with. Yes, you might see more activity going on in one area than the other, but as long as you see them and keep building up the momentum one on top of the other, you are a success.

Success is never at the end of the journey. It is always in the process of achieving your heart's desires that carries your success quotient. When you come to the end of the journey, you are empowered to start a new one. You become a coach to many others and you would in turn be living your purpose on your terms. While 21 days of following a routine forms a habit, it is the 40 days discipline that will put you on the highway to tap your true potential.

When you stop growing you start dying.

40 Day Rules

You might have observed that there are very few rules that I asked you to follow. Rules do have their merit in the short run, as it could discipline you and keep you on track. So here are a few rules to be kept in mind for the 40 day practice. Following these rules you would be less likely to give up (that is not the purpose anyway) and you can cherish your progress.

a. Allocate a certain time of the day that you are undisturbed to follow the action steps that I list out. Do your best to adhere to the time you allocate.

b. Keep a stop watch that would end with a pleasant sound. This ensures least distraction towards time.
c. If you miss a day for any reason, you need to reset the 40 day plan and you start from Day 1 again. This is very important. Remember your goal is to finish the race. Anytime you are caught in this dilemma of how to deal with a day missed (remember, it is your EGO playing its pranks), read the list you created from your heart and feel the importance of following through.

You have learnt the techniques so far. That was your training ground. Let me remind you that the whole purpose of the exercise is to see you manifest your heart's desires. It is going to be 40 days. Yes, It is a challenge to many who are not used to such discipline. But I DARE YOU to be STRONG and bury thoughts of doubt and stick to the plan no matter what. Repeat the I AM mantra and see the magic.

Many of life's failures are people who did not realize how close they were to success when they gave up – Edison

40 day Action Plan

You can spend 15 minutes or you can spend a whole hour doing this action plan, but the key point that needs to be kept uppermost is the time that is spent with total concentration. I have observed that when I sit down to do these steps, the first 5 minutes can be real turbulence. Just like a glass of muddy water takes some time to settle down to bring the clear water on top, you need to be patient enough for the mind chatter to calm down. I have also seen that when the intention is spoken loud and clear (for the first few days at least), the mind obeys. It is taming the unruly mind that brings you immense benefits in using the techniques. It seems worse before it gets better. The goal is not an empty mind but using the mind to churn out vibrations for the spiritual Universe to work in order to bring into reality in the physical Universe.

Open your journal and mark the day you begin and number the days from 1 to 40. You can use the full page, full color and print ready sheets provided in www.ultimateguidetomanifestation.com.

Here are 9 steps for the 40 day plan. Go back to the respective chambers if you need to get more clarification. I would also suggest you to write down each of your desires in the sheet provided on the site.

1. Each time you start to work the plan, begin with Alpha state. Never let any step become a mechanical routine. Let your inner child spirit be in awe for the new experiences you create.

2. Start with a feeling of gratitude. Give thanks for the wonderful life, to your mind and capacity to even be aware of the process you have started, to your loved ones (by naming them one by one), to the career you have, the house you live in, to the luxuries you currently have, to the health situations you currently facing (yes, this is important), to your friends and families, to the country where you live and all other things you can think of. Let the energy of gratitude create a spiral all around you. Build that gratitude muscle inside of you. Let the whole body feel the vibration of this energy. Take a deep breath.

The starting point of real riches is hidden in the energy of gratitude.

3. Create the intentions for the list you created. This should be almost instantaneous by this time. Take a deep breath.

4. Generate the feelings in your physical body of having accomplished the desires in your mind's eye. The more time you spend here, the better. Take a deep breath.

5. Go into the gap of silence and let the vibration of "AAAHHH" travel up and down your spine while visualizing the object of your desire being delivered to you. Take a deep breath.

6. Continue this vibration with the powerful words of "RAAAA", "LAASUNKAAN" and "KHEPERUS'AUNGKH." Take a deep breath.

Resonating with a powerful and empowering vibratory word is far superior than an intelligent understanding of its meaning.

7. Dissolve your shortcomings by going out the doorway to get Universal help and then going out to meet your alternate Self. Feel the power and come back knowing that you can achieve things effortlessly. Take a deep breath.

8. Let the words I AM THAT I AM resonate within your inner self. Follow up with the list of I AM's and consciously make this as a background music. Each time you find yourself speaking the words "want, try, hope", immediately replace it with the power of I AM. Take a deep breath.

9. End the session by taking a deep breath and mentally counting from 1 to 5, coming out slowly and opening your eyes wide awake, feeling totally refreshed and ready to take action in the outer world by looking for synchronicities, insignificant events, unexpected visitors, calls and all the Universal winks that will follow you to get you the results.

"Celebrate like a celebrity and welcome success"- Harvu

Suresh Harvu

MY EXPERIENCES SO FAR

Chapter 11

THE NINTH CHAMBER - THE MAGIC OF CELEBRATION AND SHARING

You are finally here. You did travel the path and have every reason to celebrate. I commend you, applaud for you in making your destiny work the way you designed. Not by chance, but by choice you are creating your experiences. You are either in your first few days or weeks of mastering the art of manifestation. It took me a few years to explore what works and what does not. But you have now within your mind's reach and at your fingertips all the required resources that can take your sights off the limited horizon and into the far reaching exciting shores.

It is time to celebrate, to share and give your own soul something to cherish. Celebration is a necessity. It is a way of reciprocation to all that was handed over to you, in your path to your destiny. The more you celebrate and share, irrespective of the measure of success, the more you provide the Universe with reasons to help you celebrate further.

To this date I celebrate even the smallest of success, be it a regular pay check or an unexpected amount or a day of fasting that I am not a fan of or anything that brings a joy to the heart. And lo and behold; I get more and more reasons to celebrate.

In other words, success breeds success. This is the Universal Law of Celebration.

Sharing your joys and celebrations with your loved ones and friends is a good habit to make a part of your life. Sharing is caring and always do it with an unconditional attitude. The idea of sharing is to train your mind. You are not doing it to show the world anything. You know within yourself what you have undertaken to reap the harvest of consistently grooming your inner game through the power of the chambers described in this book.

Each one of the methods you were introduced to, is in itself a huge repository of vibrational energy than can translate into external reality. Added to this, when you get the whole inner mind game tuned, you are unstoppable.

How to celebrate and share

Here are some ideas of celebration and sharing that you could use:

a. Make it a habit of recording your wishes fulfilled in your journal. Send out a message to your near and dear. Feel the excitement in your heart and bring it out in your actions.

b. Treat yourself with a gift or go ahead and give a gift to someone you care about. It need not be always an expensive one. It is the joy of giving that counts.

c. Write a note to the Universe, thanking wholeheartedly for the unlimited possibilities and the unexpected synchronicities provided to you, and visualize that message traveling to the vast emptiness. Now go ahead and file that message in your folder and name that folder as "Notes to the Universe". This folder is a reminder of the manifestation you have co-created with the Universe. Whenever your circumstances don't look like what you expect, instead of brooding over the issue, go ahead and randomly read your own notes to the Universe. This act in itself brings you clarity in thinking and has a healing response to your soul.

d. Start guiding another person and recommend some of the techniques you found useful. Do not force it on others but provide your own experiences to instill the hope and confidence for others to get a strong hold of their destiny. You become the pebble in the ocean of life that has a ripple effect way beyond your wildest imaginations.

There are less fortunate people around you who are praying in their own way. They are looking for proof that life is a fair game. You become that blessing in their life. Be empathetic when you listen to their story, and with all the love in your heart and the wisdom you have acquired, you will glorify the vibrational spiritual being you were born, in a human body.

You are now the manifestor. Let the journey begin….Namaste!!!

Suresh Harvu

MY EXPERIENCES SO FAR

Q & A

I normally get a few questions repeatedly that are related to the action steps in each of the chambers as well as the comprehensive 40 day program. The question and answers provided below are intended to clear some of them.

Q1) What is the best time to practice the steps laid out?
Ans) It is always better to start the practice before your part of the world wakes up. 5 AM or earlier is the time when your consciousness is still in the blissful state not attached to the thoughts, actions and energies that emanate from the world outside. However, any time you choose is a good time. It is good to keep time and location constant.

Q2) I am not used to sitting down for such long times as recommended. Can I do it for short periods?
Ans) Very few are actually trained to sit still. The more you practice, you get better at doing the steps. Keep a very small goal to begin with; say 3 minutes. Set the timer and at the end of 3 minutes, just get up feeling a big achievement (in reality it is!). Slowly increase this number by 3 minutes each week. Within a few weeks, you will be on your way to massive success.

Q3) Can I do the steps while driving?
Ans) I recommend not to do anything while driving except be in the energy that you have created during the morning session. The feeling of gratitude can be felt even while driving as long as it does not distract you from the road ahead.

Q4) What is the correct way to pronounce the vibratory words AAAH, LAASUNKAAN and KHEPERUS'AUNGKH?
Ans) Visit the site www.ultimateguidetomanifestation.com for an introduction on the sounds.

Q5) How do I know that I am on track for manifesting my desires?
Ans) You will be encountering events that appear for no specific reason. Keep a note of these events and affirm in your mind that the dots are being created and they are getting connected. You might take a different road to your work due to a traffic jam. You might find someone's credit card and you trace them and hand it over, or have a sudden change of job. Keep connecting the dots and have a knowing within your inner Universe that they are all being worked out for you.

Q6) I keep missing days in my 40 day plan. It is tough to start all over again.
Ans) Yes, you could be in a testing phase. In other words, the Universe is looking for your commitment and you will be aptly rewarded. Keep moving forward with more affirmations. You could be disappointed for some time, but let that not lead to discouragement and frustration. My coaching program is designed to ensure your continuity until you reach your goals.

Q7) I sometimes feel delicate to do the words when others hear them.
Ans) You need to remind yourself that it is your journey to your fulfillment. If you have others supporting your dreams and goals, great. If not, you set the pace. One year from now you will be amazed as to how others will not only get used to your vibrations but will plead you to teach them.

Q8 Can I manifest for others?
Ans) I would recommend you to first do it for your heart's desires. Your belief and conviction will be easily conveyed to others who interact with you. When you reach a stage when another human being is

positively impacted by your very presence, then yes, you can augment their effort with your vibrations.

Q9) Where can I get more help in my efforts to manifest?
Ans) I have created a 9 month program to take you from where you are now, to the point where you turn into a manifestor. Details and qualifications for this program is available in the site www.ultimateguidetomanifestation.com.

UGM Appendix A

Neuroscientists have observed a correlation between an increase of alpha brain waves and the ability to focus and increase creative thinking. When we are in a state of physical and mental relaxation, although we are aware of what is happening around us, its frequency is around 7 to 13 pulses per second. In general, during most part of our waking state, we are accustomed to using the beta brain rhythm or waves that are more chaotic that occurs when we are consciously alert, with frequencies ranging from 13 to 60 pulses per second in the Hertz scale. There are other states of consciousness that arise from Delta and Theta waves. For now, let us put together an action plan to get into the Alpha state as quickly as possible. This state is a requirement for every action step that I introduced in this book.

There is no one perfect brain state though. Each state has its own purpose and you would rather not jump from the delta state of slow sluggish mode to beta state of rapid activity. That might be dangerous. It is like you getting out of a deep slumber unwillingly and being asked to drive your car on the highway. You are in first gear with hardly any acceleration and suddenly jumping to the fourth gear of fast acceleration. We see that beta state is rapid with lot of external activity. While alpha state is a focused, calm, relaxed state that allows you to tune into the internal (spiritual) Universe. Going from alpha to beta always produces quality and amazing results. Alpha brain waves are associated with relaxed alertness, enhanced learning, creativity, peak performance, imagination, visualization and intuition.

Steps to enter the Alpha state:

- Choose a particular place in your home where you are undisturbed for the duration of your action steps recommended in this book.
- Make yourself comfortable. Try to keep your spine as erect as you possibly can without straining.
- Take 2 deep breaths and let it out while feeling the whole body relax.
- Take a deep breath again and mentally repeat and visualize as slowly as possible the number 3 three times and feel the relaxation of your body on the exhale. I have clocked a time of 10 seconds to get a good relaxation in this step and feel the energy within while relaxing.
- Take a deep breath again and mentally repeat and visualize as slowly as possible the number 2 three times and feel the relaxation of your body on the exhale.
- Take a deep breath again and mentally repeat and visualize as slowly as possible the number 1 three times and feel the relaxation of your body on the exhale.
- Relax your scalp, forehead, eyes, jaws, neck, shoulders, chest, abdomen, thighs, knees, calves, ankle, feet; all the way to the toes. Take a few seconds for each area. The way to relax is simple. Silently repeat "RELAX" a few times for each area. There could be a tingling sensation or a fine vibration on the scalp or the forehead. You might listen to your heart beats and that actually relaxes your physical heart. Be aware of all your internal organs working perfectly doing its job.
- From a count of 1 to 10 (each number representing a second), go deeper and deeper in your relaxation.
- You are now in Alpha state of mind with brain frequencies at its optimal level.
- Now go ahead with the other steps that are recommended.

Steps to enter the Beta state:

While Alpha state is where you will be in, while doing the exercises, you would need to come back to Beta state right after. This is the state of normal activity in the waking state.

When you have completed all the steps in the exercises as detailed in each chamber, do the following:

- Just sit still for a minute or two to let the energies get absorbed within your inner space.

- Mentally count slowly from 1 to 5 taking a couple of seconds for each number.

- As you reach the number 5, open your eyes wide, feeling refreshed and ready to take action to design your destiny.

About the Author

Suresh Harvu has been involved in the Manifestation Program and Energy healing in one way or another over the last 15 years. He is a Quantum Touch Practitioner which has been a boon for so many individuals, and has been successful in dealing with issues ranging from simple headache, sprained back, sprained ankles, nerve pinch to more involved issues like chest congestion, bronchitis, and emotional issues as well.

He has also helped many individuals in setting financial goals and helping them achieve through his simple straight forward way of saving and making passive income. Suresh is very passionate about his "9 week Manifestation Course" and his unique "9 Months to Jump Start Your Life" coaching program to help individuals and families reach their true potential. He has also been involved with Homeopathy for the last 35 years. He currently lives in Freehold, NJ in the United States and can be reached at sharvu63@gmail.com

www.ingramcontent.com/pod-product-compliance
Lightning Source LLC
Chambersburg PA
CBHW070544170426
43200CB00011B/2551